We Need
Construction Workers
by Lisa Trumbauer

Consulting Editor: Gail Saunders-Smith, Ph.D.

Consultant: T. J. Ferrantella, CPC, Chairman
American Institute of Constructors
Constructor Certification Commission

Pebble Books

an imprint of Capstone Press
Mankato, Minnesota

Pebble Books are published by Capstone Press
151 Good Counsel Drive, P.O. Box 669, Mankato, Minnesota 56002
http://www.capstone-press.com

1 2 3 4 5 6 08 07 06 05 04 03

Library of Congress Cataloging-in-Publication Data
Trumbauer, Lisa, 1963–
    We need construction workers / by Lisa Trumbauer.
    p. cm.—(Helpers in our community)
    Includes bibliographical references and index.
    Contents: Construction workers—Homes and buildings—Roads and bridges—
Helping communities grow.
    ISBN 0-7368-1649-6 (hardcover)
    1. Building—Juvenile literature. 2. Construction workers—Juvenile literature.
[1. Construction workers. 2. Building. 3. Occupations.] I. Title. II. Series.
TH149 .T78 2003
624′.023—dc21   2002007664

Note to Parents and Teachers

The Helpers in Our Community series supports national social
studies standards for units related to community helpers and their
roles. This book describes and illustrates the job of construction
workers. The photographs support early readers in understanding
the text. This book also introduces early readers to subject-specific
vocabulary words, which are defined in the Words to Know section.
Early readers may need assistance to read some words and to use
the Table of Contents, Words to Know, Read More, Internet Sites,
and Index/Word List sections of the book.

Table of Contents

Construction Workers. 5
Homes and Buildings. 9
Roads and Bridges. 15
Helping Communities Grow . . . 21

Words to Know 22
Read More. 23
Internet Sites 23
Index/Word List. 24

Construction workers are builders.

Construction workers
wear hard hats,
tool belts, and boots.

Some construction workers build homes and buildings.

They measure
and cut lumber.

They use hammers
to pound nails.

14

Some construction workers build roads and bridges.

They use concrete
to build the roads
and bridges.

They drive rollers, dump trucks, and bulldozers.

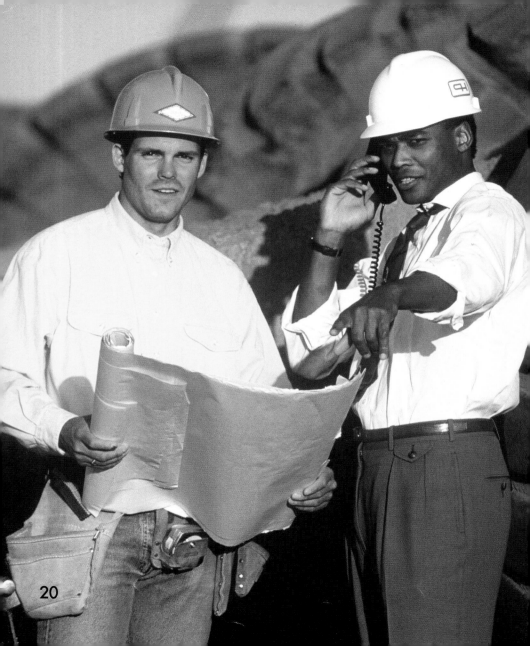

Construction workers
help communities grow.

Words to Know

bulldozer—a tractor with a big blade in front that moves soil or rock short distances

community—a group of people who live in the same area; construction workers are part of the community; they help communities grow by building new buildings, bridges, and roads.

concrete—a building material made from a mixture of sand, gravel, cement, and water

hammer—a tool with a long handle and a metal head; construction workers often use hammers to pound nails into walls and roofs.

hard hat—a large, helmet-like hat that people wear to protect their head

lumber—wood that has been processed to be used for construction

measure—to find out the size or length of an object

roller—a heavy machine that construction workers use to compact stone and other material

Read More

Deedrick, Tami. *Construction Workers.* Community Helpers. Mankato, Minn.: Bridgestone Books, 1998.

Miller, Heather. *Construction Worker.* This Is What I Want to Be. Chicago: Heinemann Library, 2002.

Schaefer, Lola M. *Construction Site.* Who Works Here? Chicago: Heinemann Library, 2000.

Internet Sites

Track down many sites about construction. Visit the FACT HOUND at *http://www.facthound.com*

IT IS EASY! IT IS FUN!

1) Go to *http://www.facthound.com*

2) Type in: 0736816496

3) Click on "FETCH IT" and FACT HOUND will find several links hand-picked by our editors.

Relax and let our pal FACT HOUND do the research for you!

Index/Word List

boots, 7
bridges, 15, 17
build, 9, 15, 17
builders, 5
buildings, 9
bulldozers, 19
communities, 21

concrete, 17
cut, 11
drive, 19
dump trucks, 19
grow, 21
hammers, 13
hard hats, 7
help, 21
homes, 9

lumber, 11
measure, 11
nails, 13
pound, 13
roads, 15, 17
rollers, 19
tool belts, 7
use, 13, 17
wear, 7

Word Count: 59
Early-Intervention Level: 10

Editorial Credits
Mari C. Schuh, editor; Abby Bradford, Bradfordesign, Inc., series designer; Molly Nei, book designer

Photo Credits
Folio, Inc./Mark Segal, 16; Richard Quataert, 18
ImageState, Inc./Jeff Smith, 4; International Stock/Patti McConville, cover
Index Stock Imagery/Mauritius, 1; Tom Ross, 6; Gary Conner, 8; Lawrence Sawyer, 10; Gary Adams, 12; Table Mesa Products, 20
Unicorn Stock Photos/Eric R. Berndt, 14

24